W9-CBQ-450

Eleanor Roosevelt

Published in the United States of America by Cherry Lake Publishing
Ann Arbor, Michigan
www.cherrylakepublishing.com

Content Adviser: Ryan Emery Hughes, Doctoral Student, School of Education, University of Michigan
Reading Adviser: Marla Conn, ReadAbility, Inc.
Book Design: Jennifer Wahi
Illustrator: Jeff Bane

Photo Credits: © FDR Presidential Library & Museum/Flickr, 5, 7, 9, 13, 15, 17, 19, 22, 23; © Lawrence Wilbur/
Library of Congress, 11; © Everett Collection Historical / Alamy Stock Photo, 21; Cover, 10, 14, 18, Jeff Bane;
Various frames throughout, Shutterstock Images

Library of Congress Cataloging-in-Publication Data

Haldy, Emma E.
  Eleanor Roosevelt / by Emma E. Haldy ; illustrated by Jeff Bane.
    pages cm. -- (My itty-bitty bio)
  Includes bibliographical references and index.
  ISBN 978-1-63470-483-0 (hardcover) -- ISBN 978-1-63470-543-1 (pdf) -- ISBN 978-1-63470-603-2 (pbk.) -- ISBN
978-1-63470-663-6 (ebook)
  1. Roosevelt, Eleanor, 1884-1962--Juvenile literature. 2. Presidents' spouses--United States--Biography--Juvenile
literature. I. Bane, Jeff, 1957- illustrator. II. Title.
  E807.1.R48H34 2016
  973.917092--dc23
  [B]
                                          2015026083

Printed in the United States of America
Corporate Graphics

About the author: Emma E. Haldy is a former librarian and a proud Michigander. She lives with her husband, Joe, and an ever-growing collection of books.

About the illustrator: Jeff Bane and his two business partners own a studio along the American River in Folsom, California, home of the 1849 Gold Rush. When Jeff's not sketching or illustrating for clients, he's either swimming or kayaking in the river to relax.

I was born in 1884.

My parents died when I was young.

My grandmother raised me.
I was lonely. I was sad.

I went to **boarding school**.
I liked learning.

Would you like boarding school?
Why or why not?

I fell in love with Franklin Roosevelt. I married him.

We had six children.

Franklin became a **politician**.
I supported his **career**.

I also helped my community.
I worked for the Red Cross.

Franklin got sick. He could not walk anymore.

I got involved in politics.
I helped Franklin. But I also had my own goals.

What are some of your goals?

Franklin was elected president of the United States.
I continued with my work.

I helped the poor. I fought **racism**. I supported education.

Franklin and I were a team.
We made America better.

When Franklin died, people
asked what I would do next.

I carried on with my work.
I gave speeches. I wrote books.

I was a **human rights** leader.

After a life of service, I died peacefully. I was buried next to Franklin.

I was a remarkable woman. I stood up for my beliefs. I fought for those in need.

What would you like to ask me?

1880

1905

Born
1884

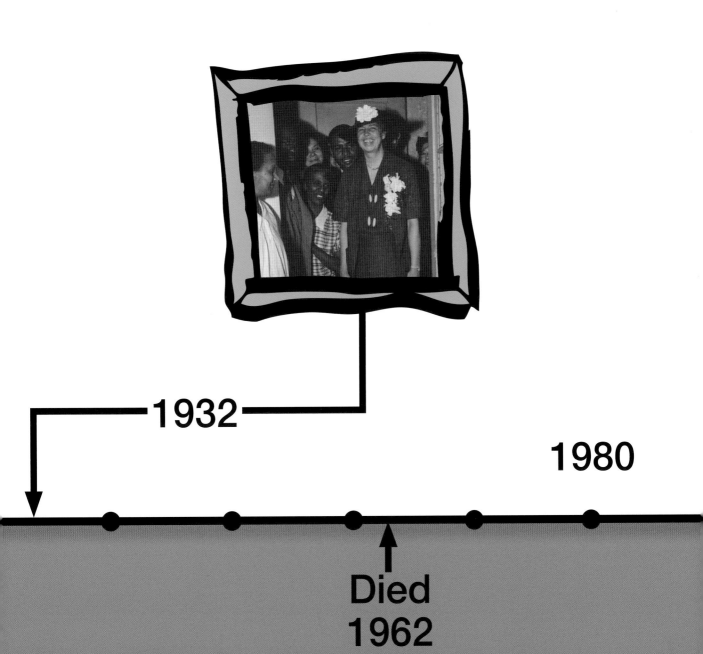

1932

1980

Died
1962

glossary

boarding school (BOR-ding SKOOL) a school that students may live in during the school year

career (kuh-REER) a person's work or jobs

human rights (HYOO-muhn RITES) rights that all people are entitled to hold, like freedom and equality

politician (pah-li-TISH-uhn) a person elected to the government

racism (RAY-siz-uhm) the belief that one race is better than another

index